W9-AVM-048

NO, THANK YOU

JANINE AMOS

Published in the United States by Windmill Books (Alphabet Soup)
Windmill Books
303 Park Avenue South
Suite #1280
New York, NY 10010-3657

Library of Congress Cataloging-in-Publication Data

Amos, Janine
     No, thank you / Janine Amos.
             p.   cm. – (Best behavior)
     Contents: Mom's cake—Too busy!—Building a palace.
     Summary: Three brief stories demonstrate how to say "No" in a polite and
friendly manner.
     ISBN 978-1-60754-022-9 (lib.) – 978-1-60754-036-6 (pbk.)
978-1-60754-037-3 (6 pack)
     1. Courtesy—Juvenile literature   2. Conduct of life—Juvenile literature
[1. Etiquette   2. Conduct of life]   I. Title   II. Series
     395.1'22—dc22

American Library Binding 13-digit ISBN: 978-1-60754-022-9
Paperback 13-digit ISBN: 978-1-60754-036-6
6 pack 13-Digit ISBN: 978-1-60754-037-3

Manufactured in China

Credits:
Editor: Louise John
Designer: Mark Holt
Photography: Gareth Boden
Production: Jenny Mulvanney

With thanks to:
Holly Gill, Charlie Horwood, Georgia Debank, Kiani Gordon, Jayden Chalmers, Jordan Burke, and Sian
and Taylar Wong.

Mom's Cake

It is snacktime. Mom has made a cake.

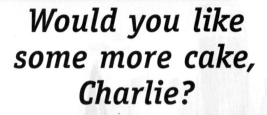

6

Mom offers the cake to Charlie.

No.

The children forget to say thank you.
How does Mom feel?

Mom offers the cake to Georgia.

How about you, Georgia?

Georgia smiles and says
No, thank you.

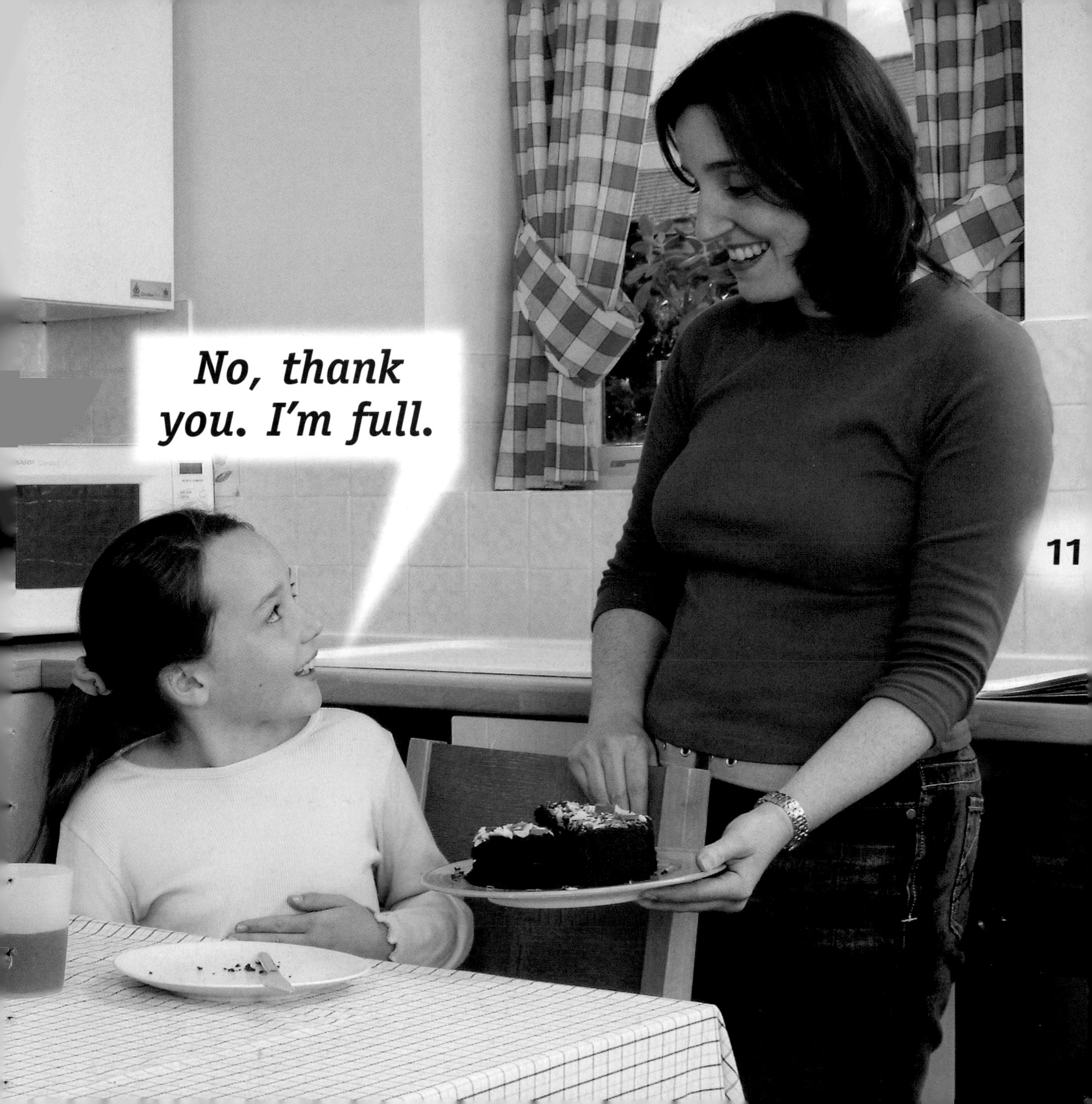
No, thank you. I'm full.

How does Mom feel now?

Too Busy!

Kiani is busy drawing.

14

Do you want to make paper planes with me?

15

Joshua comes over.

Kiani is busy.

No.

17

How does Joshua feel?

Joshua goes over to Jordan.

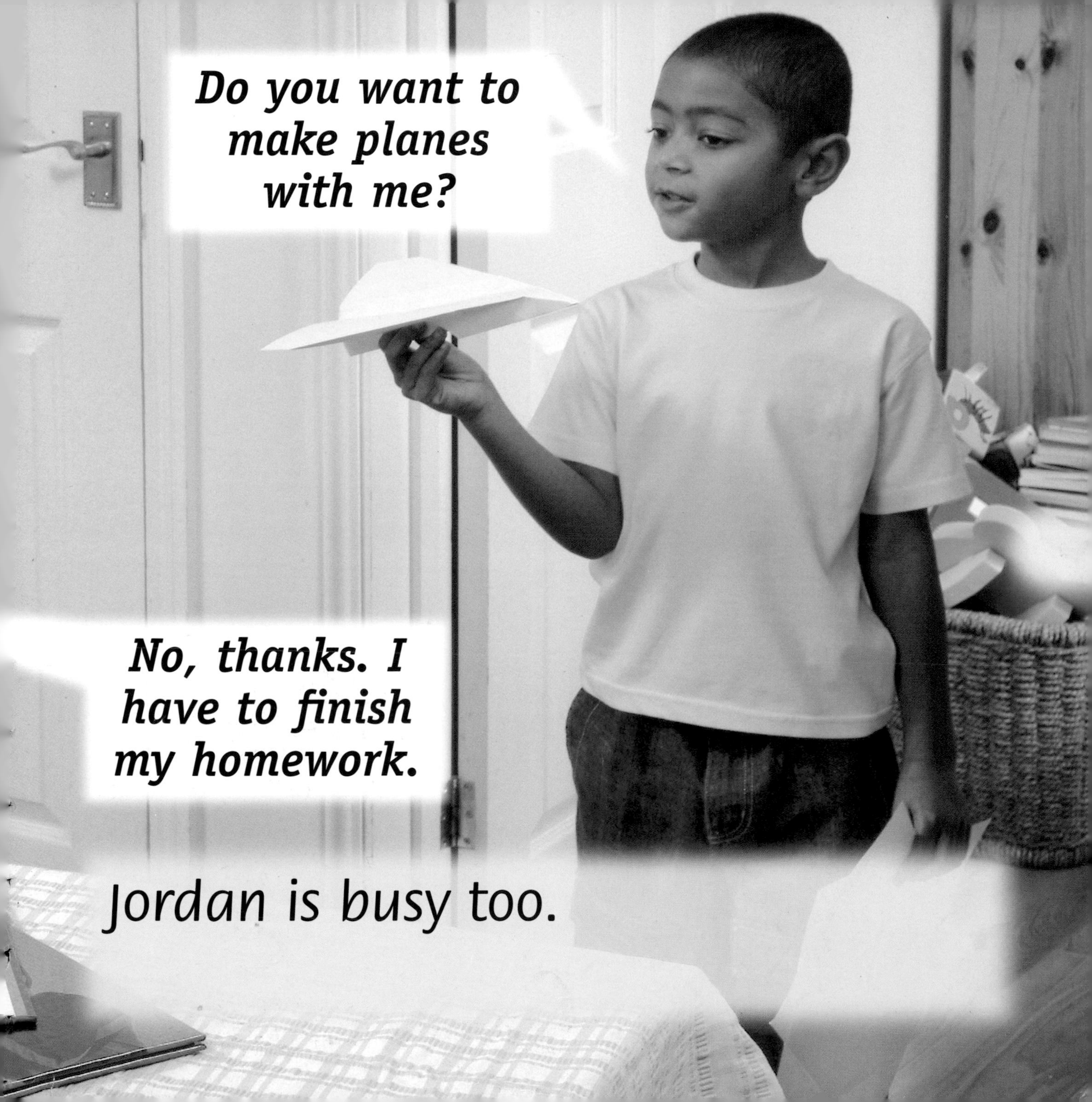

Jordan is busy too.

Building a Palace

Isobel is building a palace.

It's quite tricky.

Oops!

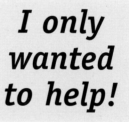

I only wanted to help!

How is Katie feeling?

Isobel thinks about it.

How does Katie feel now?

That's OK.

When you say No it can make your friends feel pushed away.

It may seem as if you don't care about them.

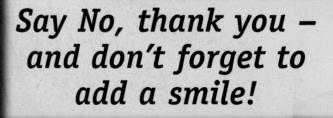

If you don't want what a friend is offering, say a friendly No.

Say No, thank you – and don't forget to add a smile!

FOR FURTHER READING

INFORMATION BOOKS

Carlson, Nancy. *How to Lose all Your Friends*. New York: Puffin, 1997.

Verdick, Elizabeth. *Words Are Not For Hurting*. Minneapolis: Free Spirit, 2004.

FICTION

Morris, Jennifer. *May I Please Have a Cookie? (Scholastic Reader)*. New York: Cartwheel Books, 2005.

AUTHOR BIO

Janine has worked in publishing as an editor and author, as a lecturer in education. Her interests are in personal growth and raising self-esteem and she works with educators, child psychologists and specialists in mediation. She has written more than fifty books for children. Many of her titles deal with first time experiences and emotional health issues such as Bullying, Death, and Divorce.